What's it like to live in ...?

Jamaica

by Ali Brownlie

HODDER
Wayland

An imprint of Hodder Children's Books

Other titles in the What's it like to live in? series:

Canada   France   Italy

For more information on this series and other Hodder Wayland titles, go to www.hodderwayland.co.uk

 © 2003 White-Thomson Publishing Ltd

Produced for Hodder Wayland by
White-Thomson Publishing
2/3 St Andrew's Place, Lewes, East Sussex BN7 1UP

Published in Great Britain in 2003 by Hodder Wayland,
an imprint of Hodder Children's Books.
This paperback edition published in 2005.

Editor: Kay Barnham
Designer: Tim Mayer
Consultant: Lorraine Harrison
Language consultant: Norah Granger – Former head teacher
and senior lecturer in Early Years Education at the
University of Brighton
Picture research: Shelley Noronha – Glass Onion Pictures

British Library Cataloguing in Publication Data
  Brownlie, Ali, 1949-
  What's it like to live in Jamaica?
  1. Jamaica - Social life and customs - Juvenile literature
  2. Jamaica - Social conditions - Juvenile literature
  I. Title II. Barnham, Kay
  306'.097292
ISBN 0 7502 4813 0

Printed and bound in China

Hodder Children's Books
A division of Hodder Headline Limited
338 Euston Road, London NW1 3BH

Picture acknowledgements
Axiom cover and 27; Sue Cunningham Photographic
(Howard J Davis) 17; Exile Images (Howard J Davis) 25;
Eye Ubiquitous (D Cumming) 9, 23, (Gavin Wickham) 22;
HWPL 4, (Howard J Davies) 6, 12, 14, 16, 18, 20, 21;
Impact Photos (Howard Sayer) 1 & 19, 15; James Davis
Travel Photography 7, 10, 24; Network (Jenny Matthews) 8,
13, 26; Topham Picturepoint 11.
Map artwork: The Map Studio.

Every effort has been made to trace copyright holders.
However, the publishers apologize for any unintentional
omissions and would be pleased in such cases to add an
acknowledgement in any future editions.

Contents

Where is Jamaica?

Jamaica is the third largest island in the Caribbean Sea. Nearly three million people live there. Its capital is called Kingston.

Many people visit the beautiful island of Jamaica every year.

People have come from all over the world to live in Jamaica. This is why there is such a mix of music, food and religion.

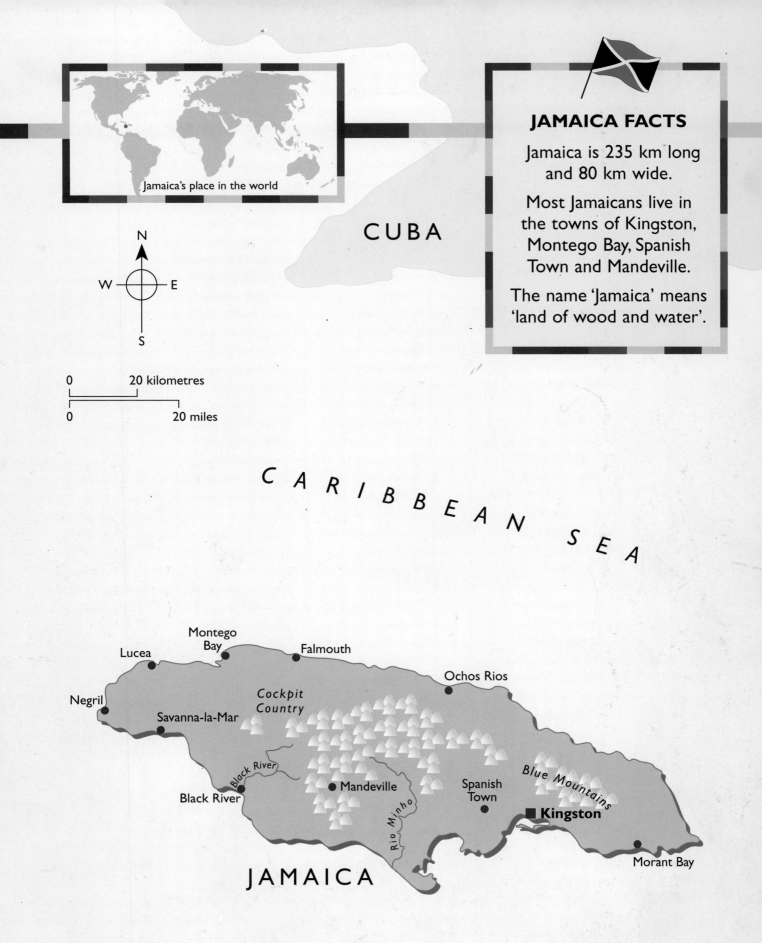

Jamaica's place in the world

N
W — E
S

0   20 kilometres

0   20 miles

CUBA

JAMAICA FACTS

Jamaica is 235 km long and 80 km wide.

Most Jamaicans live in the towns of Kingston, Montego Bay, Spanish Town and Mandeville.

The name 'Jamaica' means 'land of wood and water'.

CARIBBEAN SEA

Montego Bay
Lucea
Falmouth
Ochos Rios
Negril
Cockpit Country
Savanna-la-Mar
Black River
Black River
Mandeville
Rio Minho
Spanish Town
Blue Mountains
Kingston
Morant Bay

JAMAICA

Cities

About 750,000 people live in Kingston, the largest city. Many people from the countryside come here looking for work. Kingston has banks, office blocks and **shopping malls**.

▼

Kingston Harbour is so big that people catch the ferry from one side to the other.

Montego Bay, on the north-west coast, is the second-largest city in Jamaica. It has hotels and sandy beaches.

This plane coming in to land at Montego Bay is bringing more **tourists** to Jamaica.

The landscape

Most of Jamaica is mountainous. The mountains are covered in thick forests and are surrounded by flat coastal **plains**. Fast-flowing rivers form waterfalls as they tumble down the mountain slopes.

Coffee beans grown in the Blue Mountains are world famous.

Jamaica is surrounded by the warm, clear Caribbean Sea. The island has some of the finest beaches in the world.

▲

On the west coast, there are **coral reefs** in the shallow sea.

The weather

The Jamaican coasts are hot and **humid** all year round. However, the north coast gets more rain than the south. It is cooler in the mountains.

Trees shade this Jamaican river from the hot sun.

Strong winds and heavy rainfall can damage houses and cause **landslides** and floods.

Tropical storms and **hurricanes** can happen any time between May and November. Fewer **tourists** visit during these months.

Transport

In Jamaica, most people use minibuses that travel all over the island. Children who live in **remote** country areas go to school by minibus or walk.

Buses leave when they are full. They do not follow a **timetable**.

However, more and more people are buying their own cars and the roads and cities are getting busier.

Traffic jams are becoming more common in towns like Kingston.

Farming

Many Jamaicans work as farmers. Some of them work on **plantations** growing coffee, **sugar cane** and bananas. This produce is usually sold to other countries.

Coffee beans are washed, roasted and then packed.

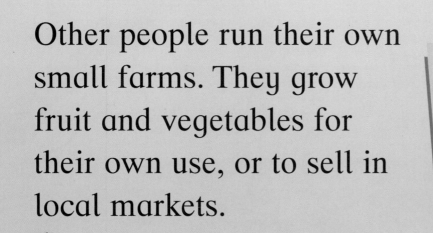

Other people run their own
small farms. They grow
fruit and vegetables for
their own use, or to sell in
local markets.

Many types of fruit
and vegetables are
grown in Jamaica.

15

Food

Jamaican food is rich, spicy and very tasty. The national dish is salt fish and a fruit called ackee. When cooked, ackee tastes a little like scrambled eggs.

Salt fish and ackee are often eaten with plantain — a fruit shaped like a banana.

Other popular **traditional** dishes are pepperpot soup, curried goat, rice, beans, chicken and brown fish stew. Sour sop juice is a kind of fruit juice.

▲

These boys are eating rice, chicken and fish at the beach.

17

Shopping

In the bigger cities, supermarkets sell a huge range of products. On the pavements, women called higglers sell homegrown fruit and vegetables.

American-style **shopping malls** are opening in the larger Jamaican cities.

In country villages there may be only one shop, but this will sell most basic things that people need to buy.

▼

This Jamaican is selling breadfruit, pineapples and other tropical fruit.

Houses and homes

Jamaica has many shanty towns. These areas are full of houses made from **recycled materials**. Some houses in the countryside still do not have running water or electricity.

Shanty towns can be very overcrowded.

Often, new houses are bought by rich **foreigners**.

Many expensive, new houses are now being built on the island. Near Kingston and Montego Bay there are large houses with swimming pools.

At work

As well as farming, many Jamaicans are **employed** in the tourist industry. They work in hotels and bars, looking after the people who visit Jamaica. Others work as guides.

Many Jamaicans earn money by making **souvenirs** for **tourists**.

The bauxite industry employs some Jamaicans. Bauxite is a valuable metal that is mined on the island. It is used to make tin cans.

Bauxite is sometimes known as 'red gold'.

Having fun

Jamaicans love music. The beat of **reggae music** can be heard all over the island. Even Jamaican pantomimes have reggae music in them.

This is a statue of Bob Marley. His music made reggae popular all over the world.

MARLEY ROAD

Jamaicans also enjoy ▲
sports such as football,
cricket, basketball and
baseball. However, young people
in particular now spend more time
playing computer games at home.

Football is one of the most popular sports in Jamaica.

25

Festivals

Most people in Jamaica are Christians. At special times like Easter or Christmas, everyone wears their best clothes and there are street dances and processions.

▲ Many Jamaicans go to church regularly.

The Independence Day
parade is full of people
wearing colourful costumes.

▲

Independence Day is on 6 August.
There is a big parade through the
streets of Kingston to the National
Stadium, where everyone celebrates
with music and dancing.

Jamaican scrapbook

This is a scrapbook of some everyday Jamaican things.

An advert for a gift shop on Montego Bay.

This is a postcard of the north-east coast of Jamaica.

Jamaicans use Jamaican dollars and cents. There are 100 cents in a dollar.

This is a Jamaican children's comic. ▶

This is an entry ticket for the Bob Marley Museum in Kingston.

These phonecards can be used in ▶ Jamaica.

Glossary

Coral reefs Skeletons of sea creatures found underwater in large, colourful groups.

Employed When someone has agreed to work for someone else.

Foreigners People who come from other countries.

Humid When the air is hot and wet.

Hurricanes Storms with very, very strong winds.

Landslides When soil becomes so wet that it slips down a hillside.

Plains Flat areas of land.

Plantations Large areas where crops are planted.

Recycled materials Things, such as wood and tin, that are used again.

Reggae music A type of music with a strong, regular beat.

Remote A place that is far away from other towns and cities.

Shopping mall A large building with lots of shops inside.

Souvenir A thing that is kept as a reminder of a place, person or event.

Sugar cane The plant that is used to make sugar.

Timetable A list of times at which events are supposed to happen.

Tourists People who are visiting a place during their holiday.

Traditional When people have done things the same way for many years.

Traffic jams When roads are so full that cars can only move very slowly.

Tropical storms Small, violent storms in the Caribbean.

Further information

Some Jamaican words

a-doors	outside
aringe	orange
bafan	clumsy
beenie	small
darkers	sunglasses
labrish	gossip
nuff	plenty
pickney	child
smadi	somebody
wamek	why
yahso	here

Books to read

The Boy from Nine Miles: The Early Life of Bob Marley by Cedella Marley and Gerald Hausman (Hampton Roads Publishing Company, 2002)

We Come from Jamaica by Ali Brownlie (Hodder Wayland, 2002)

Jamaica (Letters from Around the World) by Ali Brownlie (Cherrytree Books, 2003)

The Changing Face of the Caribbean by Ali Brownlie (Hodder Wayland, 2002)

A World of Recipes: the Caribbean by Julie McCulloch (Heinemann, 2001)

Index